# I HAVE A SISTER

# MY SISTER IS DEAF

by Jeanne Whitehouse Peterson

Pictures by Deborah Ray

Harper & Row, Publishers
New York, Hagerstown, San Francisco, London

Library of Congress Cataloging in Publication Data
Peterson, Jeanne Whitehouse.
    I have a sister—my sister is deaf.

    SUMMARY: A young girl describes how her deaf sister
experiences everyday things.
    1. Children, Deaf—Juvenile literature. 2. Children,
Deaf—Family relationships—Juvenile literature.
[1. Deaf. 2. Brothers and sisters] I. Ray, Deborah. II. Title.
HV2380.P47 1977   362.7'8'42   76-24306
ISBN 0-06-024701-0
ISBN 0-06-024702-9 lib. bdg.

To Julie Ann

JWP

To those I love

DR

I have a sister.
My sister is deaf.
She is special.
There are not many sisters like mine.

My sister can play the piano.
She likes to feel the deep rumbling chords.
But she will never be able to sing.
She cannot hear the tune.

My sister can dance with a partner or march in a line.
She likes to leap, to tumble, to roll,
to climb to the top of the monkey bars.
She watches me as we climb.
I watch her, too.
She cannot hear me shout "Look out!"
But she can see me swinging her way.
She laughs and swings backward, trying to catch my legs.

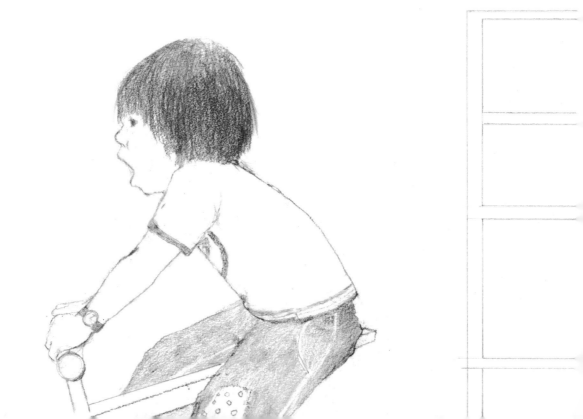

I have a sister who likes to go with me
out to the grassy lot behind our house.
Today we are stalking deer.
I turn to speak to her. I use no voice,
just my fingers and my lips.
She understands, and walks behind me,
stepping where I step.
I am the one who listens
for small sounds.
She is the one who watches
for quick movements in the grass.

When my sister was very small,

when I went to school and she did not,

my sister learned to say some words.

Each day she sat on the floor with our mother,

playing with some toys we keep in an old shoe box.

"It's a ball," our mother would say.

"It's a dog. It's a book."

When I came home, I also sat on the floor.

My sister put her hands into the box.

She smiled and said, "Ball."

*Baaaal* it sounded to me.

"It's a ball," I repeated, just like our mother did.

My sister nodded and smiled.

"Ball," she said once more.

Again it sounded like *baaaal* to me.

Now my sister has started going to my school,
although our mother still helps her speak and lip-read at home.
The teacher and children do not understand every word
she says, like *sister* or *water* or *thumb*.
Today the children in her room told me,
"Your sister said *blue!*"
Well, I heard her say that a long time ago.
But they have not lived with my sister for five years
the way I have.

I understand my sister.

My sister understands what I say too,

especially if I speak slowly and move my hands a lot.

But it is not only my lips and fingers that my sister watches.

I wore my sunglasses yesterday.

The frames are very large. The lenses are very black.

My sister made me take them off when I spoke.

What do my brown eyes say to her brown eyes?

That I would really rather play ball than play house?

That I just heard our mother call,

but I do not want to go in yet?

Yes, I have a sister who can understand what I say.
But not always.
Last night I asked, "Where are my pajamas?"
She went into the kitchen and brought out a bunch of bananas
from the fruit bowl on the table.

My friends ask me about my little sister.
They ask, "Does it hurt to be deaf?"
"No," I say, "her ears don't hurt,
but her feelings do when people do not understand."

My sister cannot always tell me with words
what she feels.
Sometimes she cannot even show me with her hands.
But when she is angry or happy or sad,
my sister can say more with her face and her shoulders
than anyone else I know.

I tell my friends I have a sister
who knows when a dog is barking near her
and who says she does not like the feel of that sound.
She knows when our cat is purring
if it is sitting on her lap,
or that our radio is playing
if she is touching it with her hand.

But my sister will never know if the telephone is ringing
or if someone is knocking at the door.
She will never hear the garbage cans
clanging around in the street.

I have a sister who sometimes cries at night,
when it is dark and there is no light in the hall.
When I try plugging my ears in the dark,
I cannot hear the clock ticking on the shelf
or the television playing in the living room.
I do not hear any cars moving out on the street.
There is nothing.
Then I wonder, is it the same?

I have a sister who will never hear the branches
scraping against the window of our room.
She will not hear the sweet tones of the wind chimes
I have hung up there.
But when the storms come,
my sister does not wake to the sudden rolling thunder,
or to the quick *clap-clap* of the shutters in the wind.
My little sister sleeps.
I am the one who is afraid.

When my friends ask, I tell them
I have a sister who watches television
without turning on the sound.
I have a sister who rocks her dolls
without singing any tune.
I have a sister who can talk with her fingers
or in a hoarse, gentle voice.
But sometimes she yells so loud,
our mother says the neighbors will complain.

I stamp my foot to get my sister's attention,
or wave at her across the room.
I come up beside her and put my hand on her arm.
She can feel the stamping. She can feel the touching.
She can glimpse my moving hand from the corner of her eye.
But if I walk up behind her and call out her name,
she cannot hear me.

I have a sister.
My sister is deaf.